WILD DOGS

AN IMAGINATION LIBRARY SERIES

by Victor Gentle and Janet Perry

Gareth Stevens Publishing

A WORLD ALMANAC EDUCATION GROUP COMPANY

Please visit our web site at: www.garethstevens.com
For a free color catalog describing Gareth Stevens Publishing's
list of high-quality books and multimedia programs,
call 1-800-542-2595 or fax your request to (414) 332-3567.

Library of Congress Cataloging-in-Publication Data

Gentle, Victor.
        Coyotes / by Victor Gentle and Janet Perry.
             p. cm. — (Wild dogs: an imagination library series)
        Includes bibliographical references and index.
        Summary: Introduces the physical characteristics and behavior of coyotes and discusses
   why ranchers dislike them even though they are helpful.
        ISBN 0-8368-3095-4 (lib. bdg.)
        1. Coyote—Juvenile literature. [1. Coyote.] I. Perry, Janet. II. Title.
    QL737.C22G4466   2002
    599.77'25—dc21   2001054950

First published in 2002 by
Gareth Stevens Publishing
A World Almanac Education Group Company
330 West Olive Street, Suite 100
Milwaukee, WI 53212 USA

Text: Victor Gentle and Janet Perry
Page layout: Victor Gentle, Janet Perry, and Tammy Gruenewald
Cover design: Tammy Gruenewald
Series editor: Catherine Gardner
Picture Researcher: Diane Laska-Swanke

Photo credits: Cover (main) © Gerald & Buff Corsi/Visuals Unlimited; cover (background)
Diane Laska-Swanke; p. 5 © John Sohlden/Visuals Unlimited; p. 7 © Tom & Pat Leeson;
pp. 9, 17, 21 © Alan & Sandy Carey; p. 11 © William Grenfell/Visuals Unlimited; p. 13
© Tom Lazar/BBC Natural History Unit; p. 15 © Thomas D. Mangelsen/BBC Natural
History Unit; p. 19 © Erwin C. Nielsen/Visuals Unlimited

Printed in the United States of America

1 2 3 4 5 6 7 8 9 06 05 04 03 02

Front cover: This coyote howls in the middle
of an open plain. Coyote howling can be heard
for miles.

TABLE OF CONTENTS

Words that appear in the glossary are printed in **boldface** type the first time they occur in the text.

GHOST DOGS

If you live in a city, you might see a strange dog running along a highway. Take a good look. The dog is sure of itself. It does not seem lost. It seems to know where it is going, and it is moving quickly. Then, before your very eyes, the dog disappears into the tall roadside weeds.

Could that strange dog really have been a coyote? Yes, coyotes live all over North America — in forests, on grasslands, near swamps, and in cities, too.

Coyotes use the easiest paths to get from one place to another. This one happily zips along a human highway.

COYOTE SONGS

Most people hear coyotes long before they see one. Coyotes howl high, and they howl low. They use many different kinds of howls. They howl during the day and late at night. They howl together, and they howl alone. They howl when they are hungry and when they find food. What do all these howls mean? We can only guess.

For now, only coyotes understand their songs. Only they know when to sing. People simply listen and wonder what the coyotes are saying or planning.

Howling looks easy. Just lean back and let go! Coyotes use other sounds, too. *Yip!* — look out! *Whine!* — I'm in trouble. *Growl!* — back off!

GOOD DOGS

Coyotes sometimes live close to cattle and sheep ranches. In fact, coyotes do a lot to help **ranchers**.

Coyotes eat **rodents** like mice that ruin grain and carry disease. They clear the land of dead and sick deer, moose, elk, and other **game**. Coyotes gobble up hundreds of grasshoppers that can eat entire grain fields, destroying all the winter food for **cattle**.

So why do ranchers and farmers worry about coyotes and kill them? Because, like us, coyotes like an easy meal.

Winter can be deadly. Food is hard to get, and the cold can kill. Here, coyotes feed on a frozen bison carcass. The coyotes have grown long, warm fur coats.

QUICK COYOTE CHOW

Coyotes like fast, easy food! They do not turn up their noses at garbage or **roadkill**. They also kill unguarded farm animals when they are easy to catch.

Often, people blame coyotes for killing animals that really were killed by disease, wolves, or hunters.

Farmers and ranchers who respect coyotes keep dogs to guard their animals. At night, these farmers put their lambs, calves, and **foals** inside a barn or pen.

Fast food can be deadly. This coyote took the bait and was trapped. People trap and kill coyotes because they think coyotes are pests.

WILY COYOTES

Cartoon coyotes may be tricky, but they work harder than real coyotes. Whenever they can, truly wily coyotes let others do the hunting.

A coyote may lie in wait as a **badger** digs for ground squirrels. Some of the squirrels escape the badger but run right into the path of the coyote. Coyotes also follow trains as they rumble past fields and then pounce on squirrels startled by the noise. Other coyotes nab mice that flee from tractors gathering up grain.

This coyote has a snack by the tail. Coyotes are very successful **predators**. They catch two out of three animals that they try for.

COYOTE CONSTRUCTION

What if no badgers, trains, or tractors are around to make hunting easy? Coyotes do what they are built to do. They hunt for themselves.

Strong hearing and a great sense of smell help coyotes find **prey**. Coyotes can hear small animals deep beneath snow and earth. Coyotes can sniff a footprint and tell which animal made it.

Long legs help coyotes dash through snowdrifts that slow down their prey. Their legs are built to pounce, helping them catch small animals totally by surprise.

Ready or not, here I come! Poised to spring on its prey, this coyote stands on its hind feet, paws and jaws at the ready.

LEADERS OF THE PACK

Coyotes **mate** in the dead of winter. In a **pack**, only the **alpha** male and female mate and have **pups**. The rest of the coyotes in the pack — usually their grown pups — help protect and babysit new pups. Coyotes that live in a pack can also hunt large animals together.

Some coyotes do not live in a pack. Lone coyotes travel long distances to mate.

Whether or not coyotes live in a pack, they usually pair up for life. Coyote couples bring food to each other, wrestle, growl, whine, and howl together.

These two coyotes may be getting to know each other by scent for the first time, or they may be together again after time apart.

PUPS AND PALS

In spring, three to six blind, fluffy coyote pups are born in a hidden place called a **den**. At first, the pups get milk from their mother. After two weeks, they open brand-new blue eyes on the world. They leave the den when they are one month old.

In summer, the pups learn to hunt by pouncing on their den pals. Soon, they go on hunting trips and snatch grasshopper snacks. If the pups are lucky, their mother brings them a live mouse for pouncing practice. If the mouse is lucky, the pups miss.

Coyote dens might be old badger holes, rotten logs, or drainage pipes. Pups like these are as small as hamsters and are easy to hide.

BETTER LIVING WITH COYOTES

There are more coyotes today than ever. Some people say that is bad news. To them, the only good coyote is a dead coyote.

Some people do not understand that killing coyotes will ruin their land. Without coyotes, animals like mice, voles, and grasshoppers will eat the grass and grain that cattle and sheep need. There will be too many weak and sick game animals.

Left alone, coyotes help keep the numbers of these animals down. The wild takes care of coyotes, and coyotes take care of the wild.

Is this pup howling for food, family fun, or its sisters and brothers? As we learn about coyotes, we might discover the answers to some wild questions.

MORE TO READ, VIEW, AND LISTEN TO

Books (Nonfiction)   *Coyote: North America's Dog.* Stephen R. Swinburne (Boyds Mills)
    Coyotes. Nature Watch (series). Cherie Winner (Carolrhoda)
    Coyotes in the Crosswalk. Diane Swanson (Voyageur)
    Wild Dogs (series). Victor Gentle and Janet Perry (Gareth Stevens)

Books (Fiction)   *At the Edge of the Forest.* Jonathan London (Candlewick)
    Coyote Steals the Blanket. Janet Stevens (Holiday House)
    Coyote Walks on Two Legs: A Book of Navajo Myths and Legends.
       Gerald Hausman (Philomel Books)
    Moon Song. Byrd Baylor (Scribner)

Books (Audio)   *Coyote at Piñon Place.* Deborah Dennard (Soundprints)

Videos (Nonfiction)   *Hot Dogs and Cool Cats.* (National Geographic Kids)
    Yellowstone National Park: Realm of the Coyote. (National Geographic)

PLACES TO VISIT, WRITE, OR CALL

Coyotes live at the following zoos. Call or write to the zoos to find out about their coyotes and their plans to preserve coyotes in the wild. Better yet, go see a coyote, person to dog!

Los Angeles Zoo
5333 Zoo Drive
Los Angeles, CA 90027-1498
(323) 644-6400

Northeastern Wisconsin Zoo
4418 Reforestation Road
Green Bay, WI 54313
(920) 448-4466

Buttonwood Park Zoo
425 Hawthorn Street
New Bedford, MA 02740
(508) 991-4556

Phoenix Zoo
455 North Galvin Parkway
Phoenix, AZ 85008
(602) 273-1341

WEB SITES

If you have your own computer and Internet access, great! If not, most libraries have Internet access. The Internet changes every day, and web sites come and go. We believe the following sites are likely to last and give the best, most appropriate links for readers to find out more about coyotes and other wild dogs around the world.

To get started finding web sites about coyotes, choose a general search engine. You can plug words into the search engine and see what it finds for you. Some words related to coyotes are: *den, howl, pack,* and *wild dogs.*

www.yahooligans.com

This is a huge search engine and a great research tool for anything you might want to know. For information on coyotes, click on Animals under the Science & Nature heading. From the animals page, you can see or hear coyotes and other wild dogs by clicking on Animal Sounds or Animal Pictures.

destertusa.com/june96/dn_cycot.html

The *DesertUSA* page has facts about the coyote, a short coyote movie, coyote noises, and a map showing where coyotes live in North America. Click on the home button, and you can also find out a lot about deserts.

www.enchantedlearning.com/subjects/ mammals/dog

At *Enchanted Learning,* you will find virtual coloring pages, games, puzzles, and more about coyotes, where they live, and the animals they live alongside, such as bears, cougars, moose, goats, and otters.

www.nationalgeographic.com/

Go to the kids page at the National Geographic Society's web site and click on Creature Features. Type in the word *coyote* to find another page with coyote videos, sounds, and a map showing where they live.

www.ngpc.state.ne.us/wildlife/coyote.html

Nebraska Wildlife's page has information about the coyote. At the bottom of the page, you will find a great coyote howl.

GLOSSARY

You can find these words on the pages listed. Reading a word in a sentence helps you understand it even better.

alpha (AL-fuh) — the leader in a pack 16

badger (BAJ-ur) — a gray, furry animal with a black-and-white head that lives underground and is active at night 12, 14, 18

cattle (KAT-uhl) — animals in a group that includes cows, bulls, and buffaloes 8, 10, 20

den (DEN) — the place where some animals give birth, hide their young, and sleep 18

foals (FOHLZ) — young horses 10

game (GAYM) — wild animals, such as deer, moose, or rabbits, hunted by people 8, 20

mate (MAYT) — to come together to make babies 16

pack (PAK) — group of coyotes 16

predators (PRED-uh-turs) — animals that hunt other animals for food 12

prey (PRAY) — animals that are hunted by other animals for food 14

pups (PUHPS) — baby coyotes 16, 18, 20

ranchers (RAN-churz) — people who work on large farms of cattle, sheep, or horses 8, 10

roadkill (ROHD-kil) — animals killed by traffic and left in the road 10

rodents (ROHD-uhnts) — small animals such as beavers, mice, squirrels, moles, and voles 8

INDEX